International Environmental Financing: The Global Environment Facility (GEF)

Richard K. Lattanzio

Analyst in Environmental Policy

June 3, 2013

Congressional Research Service

7-5700

www.crs.gov

R41165

CRS Report for Congress ———————————————————————

Prepared for Members and Committees of Congress

Summary

The United States contributes funding to various international financial institutions to assist developing countries to address global climate change and other environmental concerns. Congress is responsible for several activities in this regard, including (1) authorizing periodic appropriations for U.S. financial contributions to the institutions, and (2) overseeing U.S. involvement in the programs. Issues of congressional interest include the overall development assistance strategy of the United States, U.S. leadership in global environmental and economic affairs, and U.S. commercial interests in trade and investment. This report provides an overview of one of the oldest international financial institutions for the environment—the Global Environment Facility (GEF)—and analyzes its structure, funding, and objectives in light of the many challenges within the contemporary landscape of global environmental finance.

GEF is an independent and international financial organization that provides grants, promotes cooperation, and fosters actions in developing countries to protect the global environment. Established in 1991, it unites 182 member governments and partners with international institutions, nongovernmental organizations, and the private sector to assist developing countries with environmental projects related to six areas: biodiversity, climate change, international waters, the ozone layer, land degradation, and persistent organic pollutants. GEF receives funding from multiple donor countries—including the United States—and provides grants to cover the additional or "incremental" costs associated with transforming a project with national benefits into one with global environmental benefits. In this way, GEF funding is structured to "supplement" base project funding and provide for the environmental components in national development agendas. GEF partners with several international agencies, including the International Bank for Reconstruction and Development, the United Nations Development Program (UNDP), and the United Nations Environment Program (UNEP), among others, and is the primary fund administrator for four Rio (Earth Summit) Conventions, including the Convention on Biological Diversity (CBD), the United Nations Framework Convention on Climate Change (UNFCCC), the Stockholm Convention on Persistent Organic Pollutants (POPs), and the United Nations Convention to Combat Desertification (UNCCD). GEF also establishes operational guidance for international waters and ozone activities, the latter consistent with the Montreal Protocol on Substances that Deplete the Ozone Layer and its amendments. Since its inception, GEF has allocated $11.5 billion—supplemented by more than $57 billion in co-financing—for more than 3,200 projects in over 165 countries.

GEF is one mechanism in a larger network of international programs designed to address the global environment. Accordingly, its effectiveness depends on how the fund addresses programmatic issues, builds upon national investment plans, reacts to recent developments in the financial landscape, and responds to emerging opportunities. Critics contend that the existing system has had limited impact in addressing major environmental concerns—specifically climate change and tropical deforestation—and has been unsuccessful in delivering global transformational change. A desire to achieve more immediate impacts has led to a restructuring of the Multilateral Development Banks' (MDBs') role in environmental finance and the introduction of many new bilateral and multilateral funding initiatives. The future of GEF remains in the hands of the donor countries, including the United States, which can choose to broaden the mandate and/or strengthen its institutional arrangements or reduce and replace it by other bilateral or multilateral funding mechanisms.

Contents

Figures

Tables

Appendixes

Contacts

Introduction

Many governments acknowledge that environmental degradation and climate change pose international and trans-boundary risks to human populations, economies, and ecosystems that could result in a worsening of poverty, social tensions, and political stability. To confront these global challenges, countries have negotiated various international agreements to protect the environment, reduce pollution, conserve natural resources, and promote sustainable growth. While some observers have called upon developed countries to take the lead in addressing these issues, efforts are unlikely to be sufficient without similar measures being implemented in developing countries. Developing countries, however, focused on poverty reduction and economic growth, may not have the financial resources, technological know-how, or institutional capacity to deploy such measures. Therefore, international support for these areas has remained the principal method for governments to assist developing country action on global environmental problems.[1]

The United States and other industrialized countries have committed to financial assistance for environmental initiatives through several multilateral agreements (e.g., the Montreal Protocol (1987), the United Nations Framework Convention on Climate Change (1992), United Nations Convention to Combat Desertification (1994), and the Copenhagen Accord (2009)). International financial assistance takes many forms, from fiscal transfers to market transactions, and includes foreign direct investment (FDI), bilateral overseas development assistance (ODA), and contributions to multilateral development banks (MDBs)[2] and other international financial institutions (IFIs), as well as the offering of export credits, loan guarantees, and insurance products.

Error! Reference source not found. outlines recent U.S. financial support for multilateral environmental initiatives. Congress is responsible for several activities in this regard, including (1) authorizing periodic appropriations for U.S. financial contributions to the institutions, and (2) overseeing U.S. involvement in the programs. Issues of congressional interest include the overall development assistance strategy of the United States, U.S. leadership in global environmental and economic affairs, and U.S. commercial interests in trade and investment.[3] As Congress considers potential authorizations and/or appropriations for initiatives administered through the Department of State, the Department of the Treasury, and other agencies with international programs, it may have questions concerning the direction, efficiency, and effectiveness of current bilateral and multilateral programs. This report provides an overview of one of the oldest, largest, and most comprehensive multilateral programs to date—the Global Environment Facility (GEF)—and analyzes its structure, funding, and objectives in light of the many challenges within the contemporary landscape of global environmental finance.

---

[1] For a more detailed discussion on various sources and mechanisms of financial assistance for climate change activities, see CRS Report R41808, *International Climate Change Financing: Needs, Sources, and Delivery Methods*, by Richard K. Lattanzio and Jane A. Leggett.

[2] The group of multilateral development banks referred to in this report includes the World Bank Group (WBG), African Development Bank (AfDB), Asian Development Bank (ADB), European Bank for Reconstruction and Development (EBRD), and Inter-American Development Bank Group (IDB).

[3] For more substantive analysis of foreign aid and congressional roles, see CRS Report R40213, *Foreign Aid: An Introduction to U.S. Programs and Policy*, by Curt Tarnoff and Marian Leonardo Lawson; and CRS Report R41170, *Multilateral Development Banks: Overview and Issues for Congress*, by Rebecca M. Nelson.

Table 1. Recent U.S. Budget Authority
for Multilateral Climate and Environment Funds

In nominal US$ million

Agency/Program	2010 Enacted	2011 Enacted	2012 Enacted	2013 Enacted[a]	2014 Request
Department of State					
Least Developed Country Fund	30.0	25.0	25.0	TBD	TBD
Special Climate Change Fund	20.0	10.0	10.0	TBD	TBD
World Bank Forest Carbon Partnership	10.0	8.0	TBD	TBD	TBD
Department of Treasury					
Tropical Forests Conservation Act	26.0	16.4	12.0	12.0	0.0
Global Environment Facility	86.5	89.8	119.8[b]	129.4[c]	143.8
Climate Investment Fund: Clean Technology Fund	300.0	184.6	229.6[d]	175.3	215.7
Climate Investment Fund: Strategic Climate Fund - Pilot Program for Climate Resilience	55.0	10.0	18.7[e]	25.0[f]	34.0[g]
Climate Investment Fund: Strategic Climate Fund - Forest Investment Program	20.0	30.0	37.5[e]	12.5[f]	17.0[g]
Climate Investment Fund: Strategic Climate Fund - Scaling-Up Renewable Energy	0.0	10.0	18.7[e]	12.5[f]	17.0[g]

Source: Office of Management and Budget, *The Budget of the United States Government,* 2011, 2012, 2013, and 2014; CRS correspondence with Department of State and Department of the Treasury.

Notes: TBD, "to be determined": Appropriated funds for some programs/activities are drawn from larger line item categories in agency budget authorities, occasionally with "shall"-language implementing spending ceilings. Allocations for these programs are left at the discretion of the agency and have yet to be determined and/or fully reported.

a. Except where noted, FY2013 Enacted amount is as continuing resolution in the Consolidated and Further Continuing Appropriations Act, 2013 (P.L. 113-6). Figures do not include sequestration reduction.

b. FY2012 Enacted amount for GEF includes the transfer of $30 million from the Economic Support Fund as provided in the Consolidated Appropriations Act, 2012 (P.L. 112-74).

c. FY2013 Enacted amount for the GEF is as provided in the Consolidated and Further Continuing Appropriations Act, 2013 (P.L. 113-6).

d. FY2012 Enacted amount for CTF includes the transfer of $45 million from the Economic Support Fund as provided in the Consolidated Appropriations Act, 2012 (P.L. 112-74).

e. FY2012 Enacted amount for SCF includes the transfer of $25 million from the Economic Support Fund as provided in the Consolidated Appropriations Act, 2012 (P.L. 112-74).

f. FY2013 Enacted amount for SCF is $47.3 million for all three programs. The figures in the table reflect Treasury's internal proposal for contribution among the PPCR, FIP, and SREP.

g. FY2014 Request amount for SCF is $68.0 million for all three programs. The figures above are estimates of contributions to each program. Treasury will finalize contributions among the PPCR, FIP, and SREP in spring 2014.

The Global Environment Facility

The Global Environment Facility (GEF) is an independent and international financial organization that provides grants, promotes cooperation, and fosters actions in developing countries to protect the global environment. Established in 1991, it unites 182 member governments and partners with international institutions, nongovernmental organizations, and the private sector to assist developing countries with environmental projects related to six areas: biodiversity, climate change, international waters, the ozone layer, land degradation, and persistent organic pollutants (POPs). GEF receives funding from multiple donor countries[4]— including the United States—and provides grants to cover the additional or "incremental" costs associated with transforming a project with national benefits into one with global environmental benefits (e.g., choosing solar energy technology over coal technology meets the same national development goal of power generation but is more costly, excluding long-term environmental externalities; GEF grants aim to cover the difference or "increment" between a less costly, more polluting option and a costlier, more environmentally sound option). In this way, GEF funding is structured to "supplement" base project funding and provide for the environmental components in national development agendas. Since its inception, GEF has allocated $11.5 billion— supplemented by more than $57 billion in co-financing—for more than 3,200 projects in over 165 countries.[5]

Background

The idea for a Global Environment Facility was proposed in a September 1989 meeting of the joint International Bank for Reconstruction and Development (the World Bank)—International Monetary Fund Development Committee after recommendation by a World Resources Institute report commissioned by the United Nations.[6] The fund was established in 1991 as a pilot program within the World Bank, and many observers saw it as the beginning of an important shift in multilateral policy toward incorporating environmental concerns into development assistance. GEF, however, quickly ran into some operational challenges. These included (1) problems with communication among the implementing agencies (i.e., among the World Bank economists, the United Nations Development Program engineers, and the United Nations Environment Program environmentalists), (2) problems with differing agendas among the donor countries (i.e., between environmental idealism in Europe and economic pragmatism in the United States and United Kingdom), and (3) problems with differing perspectives among developing countries (i.e., between an emphasis on economic growth or environmental initiatives).

---

[4] See **Figure A-1** of the **Appendix** for a list of donor countries during each GEF funding, or "Replenishment," period.

[5] Information on GEF activities, organization, policies, and projects is available on its website, at http://www.thegef.org/gef/.

[6] A full overview and analysis of the history of GEF and environmental financing can be found in a number of source materials including book length studies by Inge Kaul and Pedro Conceição, *The New Public Finance: Responding to Global Challenges,* New York: Oxford University Press, 2006; Robert L. Hicks, Bradley C. Parks, J. Timmons Roberts, and Michael J. Tierney, *Greening Aid?: Understanding the Environmental Impact of Development Assistance,* New York: Oxford University Press, 2008; and several articles including Gareth Porter, Neil Bird, Nanki Kaur, and Leo Peskett, "New Finance for Climate Change and the Environment," WWF and the Heinrich Böll Foundation, 2008; Smita Nakhooda, Jon Sohn, and Kevin Baumert, "Mainstreaming Climate Change Considerations at the Multilateral Development Banks," World Resources Institute, 2005; and Smita Nakhooda, "Correcting the World's Greatest Market Failure: Climate Change and the Multilateral Development Banks," World Resources Institute, 2008.

Initially, GEF had been opposed by developing countries who believed that a program established and controlled by higher-income donor countries under the framework of the Multilateral Development Banks was not in their best interest. They remained committed to a governing structure and a cooperative partnership founded on a U.N.-style majority-based decision. After three years of debate, GEF was restructured in 1994 to address many of its institutional challenges. GEF moved out of the World Bank to become a separate and permanent institution with enhanced involvement from developing countries in decision making and implementation. A new governing structure was instituted, the first operating procedures ("the Instrument for the GEF")[7] were documented, and the funding cycle ("the GEF Replenishment") commenced. The World Bank took on the provision of the Trust Fund. The United Nations Development Program, the United Nations Environment Program, and other international organizations contributed to project development, management, and delivery.

Organizational Structure

International Agencies: GEF currently partners with 10 international agencies: the World Bank; the United Nations Development Program (UNDP); the United Nations Environment Program (UNEP); the United Nations Food and Agriculture Organization; the United Nations Industrial Development Organization; the African Development Bank; the Asian Development Bank; the European Bank for Reconstruction and Development; the Inter-American Development Bank; and the International Fund for Agricultural Development. Procedurally, the World Bank administers funding, UNDP oversees project development, and UNEP serves as the scientific and technical advisor. The remaining agencies contribute to the management and delivery of projects.

International Conventions: GEF is the primary fund administrator for four Rio (Earth Summit)[8] Conventions, including the Convention on Biological Diversity (CBD), the United Nations Framework Convention on Climate Change (UNFCCC), the Stockholm Convention on Persistent Organic Pollutants (POPs), and the United Nations Convention to Combat Desertification (UNCCD). GEF also establishes operational guidance for international waters and ozone activities, the latter consistent with the Montreal Protocol on Substances that Deplete the Ozone Layer and its amendments.

Internal Organization: GEF's main decision-making body is the GEF Council, which is an independent board of governors responsible for developing, adopting, and evaluating operational policies and programs. The Council is composed of 32 appointed members—16 from developing countries, 14 from developed countries, and 2 from among the countries of Central and Eastern Europe and the former Soviet Union. The balance between donor and recipient countries was negotiated and agreed to by Member countries after the pilot phase of the program. The Council meets approximately every six months and allows non-governmental organizations and private individuals to attend most sessions. Formal voting goes before the GEF Assembly, which is composed of representatives from all Member countries and meets every four years. During these times, the Assembly reviews general policy for operations, membership, funding, and

---

[7] The "Instrument for the Establishment of the Restructured Global Environment Facility" is the officially adopted operating procedures of GEF. See documents at http://www.thegef.org/gef/node/2552.

[8] The United Nations Conference on Environment and Development (UNCED), also known as the Rio Summit, Rio Conference, Earth Summit, and Eco '92 was a United Nations conference held in Rio de Janeiro from June 3-14, 1992, in which 172 governments participated, with 108 sending their heads of state or government, and 2,400 representatives of non-governmental organizations (NGOs), with 17,000 people at the parallel NGO "Global Forum."

amendments. The GEF Secretariat, based in Washington, DC, services and reports to the Council and the Assembly and formulates the work program, oversees implementation, and ensures that operational policies are followed.

Voting: The Assembly and the Council make decisions and adopt regulations through the process of *consensus*. GEF defines consensus as an agreement reached by all participants which includes the resolution or mitigation of all minority objections. If, in the case of the Council, all practicable efforts have been made and no consensus appears, Members may request a *formal vote*. The GEF formal vote is a double weighted majority; that is, an affirmative vote that includes both a 60% majority of the total number of Participants and a 60% majority of the total amount of contributions.[9] This format arose through a coordinated agreement between developed and developing countries in an effort to give facility to both donors and recipients in the decision-making process. A formal vote has never been taken at Council.

Funding

Replenishments: GEF is funded by donor countries, which pledge money every four years through a process known as GEF Replenishment. The process of Replenishment was designed to allow for program flexibility, strategic planning, and periodic performance evaluations. The original GEF pilot program of $1 billion has been replenished five times with $2.01 billion in 1994, $2.67 billion in 1998, $2.93 billion in 2002, $3.13 billion in 2006, and $4.34 billion in 2010.[10] Financial commitments by donor country to the GEF pilot program and the five GEF replenishments can be found in **Figure A-1** of the **Appendix**.

U.S. Commitments: The United States supported the establishment of GEF in 1991. While the United States did not provide direct funding to the pilot phase of the program (1991-1993),[11] it has made commitments and contributions to all five GEF replenishments. U.S. commitments to the various four-year Replenishment cycles have been $430 million in 1994, $430 million in 1998, $430 million in 2002, $320 million in 2006, and $575 million in 2010, for a total of $2.185 billion. U.S. commitments correspond to 13.9% of total contributions for GEF during the history of the program, or, more specifically, 21.3% of total contributions for GEF-1, 16.1% for GEF-2, 14.7% for GEF-3, 10.2% for GEF-4, and 13.2% for GEF-5.[12]

U.S. Contributions: Payments made by the U.S. Treasury to the International Bank for Reconstruction and Development (the World Bank) as trustee for GEF have varied widely over the years due mainly to budget trends. Recent contributions include the following:

- **For FY2010**, P.L. 111-117 was enacted in December 2009 with a budget authority of $86.5 million to GEF, of which $80 million was for the final GEF-4 contribution and $6.5 million was for a portion of arrears.

---

[9] For the purpose of voting power, total contributions consist of the actual cumulative contributions made to the GEF Trust Fund.

[10] Replenishment figures calculated in Special Drawing Rights (SDRs) from respective currencies at time of pledge. Figures are nominal. GEF's fiscal year runs from July 1 to June 30.

[11] During the GEF pilot phase, the United States had a separate co-financing arrangement administered by USAID.

[12] The percentage of total contributions and the percentage of new donor funding are computed from different totals. U.S. percentage of new donor funding, including supplemental contributions, is 21.3%, 21.7%, 19.5%, 14.0%, and 16.2%, respectively. See **Appendix**, **Figure A-1**, for a full breakdown of U.S. contributions in relation to other sources.

- **For FY2011**, the U.S. Budget for Fiscal Year 2011, released in February 2010, had originally set forth a U.S. commitment of $680 million for the Fifth Replenishment, to be paid in four equal installments of $170 million from FY2011 through FY2014. The FY2011 Budget had included $170 million for the first installment of GEF-5 and $5 million for a portion of U.S. arrears, for a total request of $175 million.[13] However, in reaction to lower-than-expected pledge levels by other donor countries during the GEF-5 negotiations in May 2010, the U.S. delegation reduced its pledge to $575 million, to be paid in four equal installments of $143.75 million from FY2011 through FY2014. The U.S. pledge represents an 80% increase over the GEF-4 Replenishment. The increased pledge was precipitated in part by the U.S. Administration achieving certain policy reforms designed to improve GEF's overall effectiveness, particularly with regard to country-owned business plans for funding and resource allocation. P.L. 112-10 was enacted in April 2011 with budget authority of $89.82 million to GEF, some $53.93 million in arrears of the FY2011 pledge.

- **For FY2012**, P.L. 112-74 was enacted in December 2011 with a budget authority of $89.82 million to GEF, some $53.93 million in arrears of the FY2012 pledge. However, P.L. 112-74 included a provision under "Economic Support Fund" "that in consultation with the Secretary of the Treasury, the Secretary of State may transfer up to $200,000,000 of the funds made available under this heading to funds appropriated in this Act under the headings 'Multilateral Assistance, Funds Appropriated to the President, International Financial Institutions' for additional payments to such institutions, facilities, and funds enumerated under such headings." The Administration used this provision to transfer an additional $30 million to the GEF in FY2012.

- **For FY2013**, P.L. 113-6 was enacted in March 2013 with a budget authority of $129.4 million to GEF, some $14.35 million in arrears of the FY2013 pledge.

- **For FY2014**, the U.S. Budget for Fiscal Year 2014, released in April 2013, requested $143.75 million for the FY2014 contribution to GEF, equivalent to the FY2014 pledge.

Arrears: As of September 2012, direct payments to the trustee of GEF have totaled close to $1.8 billion over the past two decades. Further, in July 2011, the United States had cleared a portion of its GEF-3 arrears in the amount of $11.9 million through a retroactive early encashment of its GEF-4 contributions.[14] With these payments, the United States is currently $258.9 million in arrears of its pledged commitments. As of the latest "Trustee Report" furnished to GEF in November 2012, the United States is joined in arrears status by three other countries: Egypt ($0.8 million), Nigeria ($1.0 million), and Spain ($3.1 million).[15]

A summary of U.S. commitments and contributions to GEF is shown in **Table 2**. The financial status of the GEF Trust Fund and the summary of arrears by country can be found in **Figure A-2** of the **Appendix**.

---

[13] Office of Management and Budget, *The Budget of the United States Government*, 2011.

[14] "Early encashment" is a payment mechanism used by GEF that allows donors to account for interest made on their contributions.

[15] See GEF, "Global Environment Facility Trust Fund Financial Report," GEF/C.43/Inf.08, September 30, 2012, at http://www.thegef.org/gef/council_document/gef-trust-fund-financial-report.

Table 2. U.S. Commitments and Contributions to GEF by Fiscal Year

Fiscal Year	$ Committed to GEF ($ in millions, nominal)	$ Contributed to GEF ($ in millions, nominal)
1994	$0	$30.0
1995	$107.5	$90.0
1996	$107.5	$35.0
1997	$107.5	$35.0
1998	$107.5	$47.5
1999	$107.5	$167.5
2000	$107.5	$35.8
2001	$107.5	$107.8
2002	$107.5	$100.5
2003	$107.5	$146.8
2004	$107.5	$138.4
2005	$107.5	$106.7
2006	$107.5	$79.2
2007	$80.0	$79.2
2008	$80.0	$81.1
2009	$80.0	$80.0
2010	$80.0	$86.5
2011[a]	$143.8	$89.8
2012	$143.8	$119.8
2013[b]	$143.8	$129.4
2014	$143.8	TBD
Total	**$2,185.2**	**$1,786.0**

Source: CRS correspondence with U.S. Department of the Treasury.

a.   The enacted FY2011 figure includes the 0.2% rescission across all non-defense accounts, in accordance with Section 1119(a) of P.L. 112-10.

b.   The enacted FY2013 figure does not include sequestration reductions.

Congressional Jurisdiction: All U.S. funding is subject to annual congressional approval. Authorizing legislation is managed by the House Financial Services Committee and Senate Foreign Relations Committee. The House and Senate Appropriations Subcommittees on State, Foreign Operations, and Related Programs have jurisdiction over appropriations.

Project Areas

GEF funding is provided to recipient countries for projects and programs in six areas: biodiversity, climate change, international waters, ozone layer depletion, land degradation, and persistent organic pollutants. For examples of the types of projects funded by GEF, see the text box below.

Biodiversity: GEF is the financial mechanism of the 1992 United Nations Convention on Biological Diversity. The goal of GEF's program is the conservation and sustainable use of biodiversity, the maintenance of the ecosystem goods and services that biodiversity provides to society, and the fair and equitable sharing of the benefits arising out of the use of genetic resources. To achieve this goal, the program has several objectives including sustainability initiatives in protected areas, conservation measures in production sectors, capacity building to implement the Cartagena Protocol on Biosafety (CPB), and capacity building to support the implementation of the Bonn Guidelines on Access to Genetic Resources. Biodiversity projects constitute the largest percentage of GEF's portfolio, making up 36% of total grants.

Climate Change: As the financial mechanism of the 1992 United Nations Framework Convention on Climate Change, GEF allocates and disburses funding for projects in climate change mitigation (i.e., reducing or avoiding greenhouse gas emissions in the areas of renewable energy, energy efficiency, and sustainable transport), and climate change adaptation (i.e., increasing resilience to the adverse impacts of climate change of vulnerable countries, sectors, and communities). GEF projects in climate change help developing countries contribute to the overall objective of the UNFCCC to achieve a "stabilization of greenhouse gas concentrations in the atmosphere at a level that would prevent dangerous anthropogenic interference with the climate system." Moreover, GEF manages two special funds under the UNFCCC—the Least Developed Countries Fund, to assist in adaptation strategies for the most vulnerable countries; and the Special Climate Change Fund, to assist in mitigation and adaptation programs for countries that are heavily reliant of fossil-fuel technologies.

International Waters: GEF's international waters focal area does not serve as a financial mechanism for a specific convention. Through an association with regional agreements, it targets trans-boundary water systems, such as river basins with water flowing from one country to another, groundwater resources shared by several countries, and marine ecosystems bounded by more than one nation. GEF grants help countries collaborate with their neighbors to modify human activities that place stress on trans-boundary water systems and interfere with downstream uses of those resources. Some of the issues addressed include trans-boundary water pollution, over-extraction of groundwater resources, unsustainable exploitation of fisheries, control of invasive species, and balancing the competing uses of water resources.

Ozone Layer Depletion: GEF, in partnership with the 1985 Vienna Convention for the Protection of the Ozone Layer and the 1987 Montreal Protocol on Substances that Deplete the Ozone Layer, has aimed to safeguard the earth's protective ozone layer after the discovery that certain compounds were found to deplete it, posing substantial risks to human health and the environment. GEF has allocated funds to assist in phasing out ozone-depleting substances (ODS) and curbing the rising production and use of hydrochlorofluorocarbons (HCFCs). GEF's aim is to protect human health and the environment by assisting countries in phasing out consumption and production of ODS while enabling alternative technologies and practices, according to countries' commitments under the Montreal Protocol. The long-term goal of GEF interventions is to contribute to the return of the ozone layer to pre-1980 levels.

Examples of GEF Projects

I. Rural Electrification and Renewable Energy Development in Bangladesh (GEF ID 1209)

GEF Grant: $8,540,000

Description: The project promoted solar energy in rural areas by (1) increasing awareness of Solar Heating Systems (SHS) among consumers and providers; (2) building technical and management capacity; (3) implementing and evaluating SHS programs; (4) providing technical and business development support to institutions; (5) introducing standards and programs for testing and certification; (6) financing grants to buy-down capital costs to increase affordability of SHS; (7) promoting electricity as a means for income generation and social wellness; and (8) identifying mechanisms to promote sustainability. Multiple approaches to SHS delivery were enacted, including a "fee-for-service" program through rural electricity cooperatives, purchase supported by micro-credit through NGOs and microfinance lenders, and hire-purchase/direct sale programs by private dealers and NGOs. Over 40,000 systems were installed supplying energy to rural dispersed communities.

2. Biodiversity Conservation in Cacao Agro-Forestry in Costa Rica (GEF ID 979)

GEF Grant: $750,000

Description: The project improved management of cacao-based indigenous small-farms according to both ecological and organic productive principles so as to ensure conservation and sustainable use of plant and animal diversity and provide a sustainable source of family income. The project promoted and maintained on-farm biodiversity while improving livelihoods of organic cacao producers (including indigenous, Latin-mestizos, and Afro-Caribbean groups) in the Talamanca-Caribbean corridor in Costa Rica.

3. Prevention and Management of Marine Pollution in the East Asian Seas in Indonesia (GEF ID 396)

GEF Grant: $8,025,000

Description: The project developed policies and plans to control marine pollution from land and sea-based sources, upgraded national and regional infrastructures and technical skills, and established financing instruments to project sustainability. Project included selection of demonstration sites, establishment of regional monitoring and information networks, and involvement of regional association of marine legal experts to improve capacity to implement relevant conventions.

Source: GEF Project database at http://www.thegef.org/gef/gef_projects_funding (accessed November 30, 2011).

Notes: As of May 24, 2013, there were 3,404 projects listed in the GEF database, of which 2,783 were approved national projects and 621 were approved regional and global projects.

Land Degradation: In 2002, the GEF Assembly expanded GEF's mandate by adding land degradation to the portfolio and designating it the financial mechanism of the United Nations Convention to Combat Desertification. GEF focuses on sustainable agricultural practices (e.g., crop diversification, crop rotation, water harvesting, and small-scale irrigation schemes), sustainable rangeland management, and the preservation of viable indigenous forests and woodlands. GEF projects aim to integrate sustainable land management into national development priorities, and to strengthen human, technical, and institutional capacities.

Persistent Organic Pollutants: GEF is the interim financial mechanism of the 2001 Stockholm Convention on Persistent Organic Pollutants, a global and legally binding agreement to reduce and eliminate pollutants including pesticides (e.g., DDT and mirex) and industrial chemicals (e.g., PCBs) as well as unintentionally produced POPs (e.g., dioxins and furans). GEF's involvement in tackling the threats posed by POPs dates back to 1995, with the introduction of the International Waters Operational Strategy and its contaminant-based component. In this framework, GEF began to develop a portfolio of strategically designed projects including regional assessments and pilot demonstrations that addressed a number of pressing POPs-related issues.

Current Issues

Each year, billions of dollars in environmental aid flow from developed country governments—including the United States—to developing ones. GEF is one mechanism in the larger network of international programs designed to address environmental issues. While the efficiency and the effectiveness of these programs are of concern to donor country governments, a full analysis of the purposes, intents, results, and consequences behind these financial flows has yet to be conducted.[16] International relations, comparative politics, and developmental economics can often collide with environmental agendas. Critics contend that the existing system has had limited impact in addressing major environmental concerns—specifically climate change and tropical deforestation—and has been unsuccessful in delivering global transformational change. A desire to achieve more immediate impacts has led to a restructuring of the Multilateral Development Banks' role in environmental finance and the introduction of many new bilateral and multilateral funding initiatives.

The effectiveness of GEF depends on how the fund addresses its programmatic issues, reacts to recent developments in the financial landscape, and responds to emerging opportunities. The future of GEF remains in the hands of the donor countries that can choose to broaden the mandate and strengthen its institutional arrangements or to reduce and replace it by other bilateral or multilateral funding mechanisms. The following section investigates some of the current strengths and challenges facing GEF and summarizes some of the responses initiated by the program.

External Challenges for GEF

- *Rise of Climate Change Issues and Funding:* The past decade has seen a rise in the significance of global environmental issues—particularly climate change—on the political agendas of many countries. Proposed policies have not only attempted to address the environmental implications of greenhouse gas mitigation and climate change adaptation, but have become linked to energy and infrastructure issues through international economic, trade, and geo-political concerns. To address these issues, governments have begun to incorporate many global environmental objectives into their sustainable growth and development strategies. Funding for these activities has increased, and various institutional responses for this extensive portfolio are under consideration. Some critics contend that existing environmental funds (e.g., GEF) are unsatisfactory because they do not have experience managing investments of this scope.

- *The Changing Role of Multilateral Development Banks in Environmental Funding:* Multilateral Development Banks (MDBs) are key actors in the global system of environmental financing. As commercial lending institutions, some have argued that they dispense funds more efficiently than many institutional programs such as GEF; but as primary mechanisms for economic development, their past environmental lending practices have produced perceived conflicts of interest.[17] Objectives began to shift in 2005 when MDBs were encouraged by the

---

[16] See Hicks, et al., op. cit., for an initial foray into a quantified analytic and a discussion on the metrics involved.

[17] The development portfolios of most MDBs strongly emphasize a bias toward conventional fossil fuel power generation and infrastructure loans that often worked counter to environmental aims (e.g., the World Bank loaned more than $2.5 billion for conventional power projects in 2005 compared to $109 million for renewable energy or energy (continued...)

G-8 leaders to play a more leading role in sustainable development and environmentally friendly technologies.[18] Since this time, MDBs have launched many new initiatives to address the environment, including efforts to (1) account for GHG emissions and improve energy efficiency; (2) support renewable energy; (3) manage forests sustainably; (4) promote carbon finance; and (5) adapt to climate change.[19] GEF programs now find themselves in competition with many of the new initiatives in MDB portfolios.

- *Increase in New Bilateral, Multilateral, and Private Funding Mechanisms:* Many donor governments perceive that the existing environmental finance system has not produced satisfactory results.[20] In searching for new and effective approaches to environmental funding, donors have sought options that can be organized quickly, administered directly, and be demonstrated to produce a more significant impact on the environment. Many have turned to highly specified multilateral programs, bilateral or even private sector measures to accomplish these aims, and no fewer than 15 environmental finance mechanisms have been announced since 2007. GEF is in competition with many of these new initiatives for a share of environmental funding.[21]

Internal Challenges for GEF

- *Low Level of Funding by Donor Countries:* Donor countries never intended GEF to cover all the financing needed to achieve developmental objectives. Rather, it was designed to be a catalyst for additional measures to address global environmental problems. As such, historical funding provided by donor countries was never at the level required to produce significant progress in reversing global threats. This experience has demonstrated that the initial assumptions underlying GEF—that relatively small amounts of incremental grant financing could leverage multilateral investment for transformational change—may be flawed.

(...continued)

efficiency). See Gareth Porter, et al., op. cit., for further comments.

[18] See the Gleneagles Plan of Action at the 2005 G-8 Meeting in Gleneagles, Scotland. It should be noted that the portfolios of many MDBs still retain significant provisions for conventional power and infrastructure projects as compared to most bilateral environmental aid, albeit with a greater ratio of renewable and efficiency resources than in the past. See Hicks, et al., op. cit.

[19] For a full analysis of the rise of MDBs in environmental finance, see Smita Nakhooda, *Correcting the World's Greatest Market Failure: Climate Change and the Multilateral Development Banks,* World Resources Institute, 2008.

[20] Statistics confirm these perceptions: as a point of comparison, the success rate for multilaterally funded environmental projects often pales in comparison to education, health, or infrastructure projects. Only 25% of World Bank-financed environmental projects during the years 2001-2003 received a "satisfactory" project outcome rating, compared to 100% for education, 86% for health, and 87% for infrastructure. See Hicks, et al., op. cit., p.6.

[21] Recent initiatives include the Global Climate Change Alliance (GCCA) of the European Commission; the International Window of the Environmental Transformation Fund (ETF-IW) of the United Kingdom; the Spanish Millennium Development Goals (MDG) Fund; the Japanese Cool Earth Partnership; the German International Climate Initiative; the Norwegian Agency for Development Cooperation (NORAD) Rainforest Initiative; the Australian Global Initiative on Forests and Climate (GIFC); the German Life Web Initiative; the World Bank Forest Carbon Partnership Fund (FCPF); the GEF Tropical Forest Account (TFA); the World Bank Clean Technology Fund (CTF); the GEF-IFC Earth Fund; the World Bank Strategic Climate Fund (SCF) and Pilot Program for Climate Resilience (PPCR); the Kyoto Protocol Adaptation Fund; and the Copenhagen Accord Green Fund. For an analysis and overview of these new programs, see Porter, et al., 2008, op. cit.

- *Limits of Grant-based Instruments:* GEF was set up mostly to finance grants. Grants have proven to be inefficient in many development contexts given the greater leveraging and enhanced financial sustainability obtained from loan-based instruments. Such loans also provide reflows which can be lent again.

- *Difficulties in Defining "Incremental" and "Additional":* As stipulated in the "GEF Instrument," grants cover the "incremental" or "additional" cost of "transforming a project with national benefits into one with global environmental benefits." Incremental cost calculations have also been used as preference in project selection. Historically, GEF's implementing agencies have had difficulty producing a coherent methodology for calculating incremental cost, slowing the rate of project development. Furthermore, countries continue to argue over the requirements of additionality (i.e., whether or not the global environmental elements of a project would have taken place in the absence of GEF funding).

- *Difficulties with Adaptation:* GEF was established to finance global environmental benefits, which has made it difficult to justify GEF financing of climate change adaptation projects, which moreover provide local benefits.

- *Inefficient Procedures and Legal Status:* GEF's two-layer structure means that all funding must be approved twice (by GEF and the relevant GEF Agency), leading to inefficiencies. GEF's lack of legal status (the trust is held by the World Bank) prevents it from disbursing funding directly to countries with a one-step approval process.

- *Slowness of GEF Project Initiation and Implementation:* Since its inception, most note that GEF's project approval process has been long and complex. A 2006 internal report found a 66-month lapse between entry of a concept into the project pipeline and its initiation. Significant effort has been exerted to reduce the duration of the approval process, and the interval currently stands at 16 to 22 months. Bureaucratic structures, work program frequencies, Council deliberations, and consensus politics have all factored into delays.

- *Lack of Strategic Approach:* Historically, GEF has adhered to a project-by-project approach to allocating funds, wherein over 95% of pledges have been allocated to individual countries and less than 5% have been set aside for regional or global programs. The dynamic assumes that ongoing negotiations and incremental adjustments could foster transformational change in economies over time. While a project-by-project approach has allowed GEF to fulfill the mandates of many of its conventions, large-scale environmental issues such as climate change and biodiversity may demand more strategic and programmatic funding modalities.

- *Unsuccessful History of Leveraging the Private Sector:* While GEF has long recognized a need to mobilize investment resources in the private sector, successful collaboration may require a degree of experience and commitment that GEF cannot achieve under its existing structure. The length and uncertainty inherent in the GEF project cycle may make participation less attractive to the private sector, and the organization's emphasis on government entities at the expense of forming relationships with investors and manufacturers may serve as a further impediment.

GEF Reforms

GEF 4

During the 2006 Replenishment meetings, GEF worked to address many of its program deficiencies. The Council aimed to streamline costs and management fees, ensure project quality upon proposal, and reduce the length of the project pipeline. A *Sustainability Compact* was enacted that would oversee several issues, including (1) the shift away from a project-oriented approach to a strategic and programmatic one; (2) a concentration on financing pre-market innovation in an attempt to leverage private capital; (3) a heightened dedication to transparency, accessibility, and equitability; and (4) a renewed focus on country-driven ownership through the implementation of a Resource Allocation Framework (RAF) wherein funding is determined by a country's potential to generate global environmental benefits and its capacity to successfully implement GEF projects. Further, in 2007, GEF initiated a pilot public-private partnership (PPP) initiative called the "Earth Fund" to enhance engagement with the private sector. Internal assessment of these reforms has shown promise.[22]

GEF 5

Meetings leading up to the Fifth Replenishment of GEF in 2010 saw the development of policy recommendations along two lines:

1. *Enhancing Country Ownership:* A key finding in GEF's recent performance evaluation was the relationship between country-driven strategic development and project success rate. Recommendations to strengthen country ownership include (1) reforming in-country corporate programs to include greater project portfolio identification and enhanced stakeholder coordination, (2) developing a more flexible and transparent resource allocation framework, and (3) broadening access to the GEF partnership to include national development agencies in developing countries.[23]

2. *Improving the Effectiveness and Efficiency of GEF Partnerships:* Recommendations to strengthen GEF partnerships include (1) enhancing accountability to the conventions and protocols; (2) streamlining the project cycle and refining the programmatic approach; (3) enhancing engagement with the private sector; (4) implementing the results-based management framework; (5) clarifying the roles and responsibilities of GEF entities, agencies, and conventions; and (6) enhancing engagement with civil society organizations.

GEF 6

Meetings for the Sixth Replenishment of GEF began on April 3, 2013, and continue on September 10, 2013. Policy recommendations are currently under development.

---

[22] See GEF's "Fourth Overall Performance Study" and "Policy Recommendations for the Fifth Replenishment of the GEF Trust Fund," February 12, 2010, p. 4, at http://www.thegef.org/gef/node/2483.

[23] These policy recommendations correspond to those highlighted in the U.S. Budget for Fiscal Year 2011 contributing to the U.S. pledge increase for the GEF-5 Replenishment, p. 862.

Appendix. Global Environment Facility Trust Fund

Figure A-1. Commitments to GEF Pilot Phase and Replenishments

Instrument for the Establishment of the Restructured
Global Environment Facility

GLOBAL ENVIRONMENT FACILITY TRUST FUND
PILOT PHASE

COMMITMENTS AS OF APRIL 30, 2007 **
(IN MILLIONS)

Contributing Participants	Pilot Phase SDR	Total Contributions Contribution[a]	Currency
Australia	9.68	16.40	AUD
Austria	26.02	29.07	EUR e
Belgium	5.00 b	5.00	SDR c
Brazil	4.00	4.00	SDR c
Canada	6.33	10.00	CAD
China	4.00	4.00	SDR c
Côte d'Ivoire	2.00	2.00	SDR c
Denmark	16.25	16.25	SDR c
Egypt	4.00	4.00	SDR c
Finland	20.44	17.66	EUR e
France	110.08	123.00	EUR e
Germany	110.02	122.85	EUR e
India	4.00	4.00	SDR c
Indonesia	4.00	4.00	SDR c
Italy	65.14	54.23	EUR e
Japan	27.36	5,373.00	JPY
Mexico	4.00	5.48	USD
Netherlands	37.74	37.74	SDR c
Nigeria	4.00	4.00	SDR c
Norway	19.56	165.00	NOK
Pakistan	4.00	4.00	SDR c
Portugal	4.50	4.50	SDR c
Spain	10.00	10.00	SDR c
Sweden	24.54	196.07	SEK
Switzerland	30.06	30.06	SDR c
Turkey	4.00	4.00	SDR c
United Kingdom	54.73	40.30	GBP

1. New Funding from Donors	615.45	
2. Contribution from IBRD Net Income	20.92	
Total (1 + 2)	636.37 d	

** Based on Instruments of Commitments or Qualified Instruments of Commitment received by the Trustee.

a Calculated by converting the SDR amount to currency of contribution using an average daily exchange rate over the period from July 1, 1990 to Sep. 30, 1990.

b Contributing Participants had the option of taking a discount or credit for acceleration of encashment and; (i) including such credit as part of their basic share; (ii) counting such credit as a supplemental contribution; or (iii) taking such discount against the national currency contribution. Belgium opted to take a discount against their national currency contribution.

c These Contributing Participants denominated their contributions in SDRs.

d This is equivalent to USD 871.83 million using the agreed reference exchange rates for the GEF Pilot Phase

e The contributions of these Contributing Participants that are member states of the European Economic and Monetary Union (EMU) were originally pledged in each of their legacy currencies. The Trustee converted these legacy currencies into EUR, the common currency for the EMU, in January 2000 at fixed conversion rates.

Instrument for the Establishment of the Restructured
Global Environment Facility

UPDATE TO GLOBAL ENVIRONMENT FACILITY TRUST FUND
FIRST REPLENISHMENT OF RESOURCES [1]

COMMITMENTS AS OF APRIL 30, 2007 **
(IN MILLIONS)

Contributing Participants	Calculated Basic Contributions (%)^a	Calculated Basic Contributions SDR	Supplemental Contributions SDR	Additional Supplemental Contributions SDR	GEF-1 Total Contributions SDR	GEF-1 Total Contributions Contribution^b	GEF-1 Total Contributions Currency	
Argentina	–	3.57			3.57	5.00	USD	
Australia	1.46%	20.84			20.84	42.76	AUD	
Austria	0.90%	12.85	1.05	0.37	14.28	16.82	EUR	c
Bangladesh	–	2.00			2.00	2.00	SDR	d
Belgium	1.55%	22.13	0.73		22.86	27.27	EUR	c
Brazil	–	4.00			4.00	4.00	SDR	d
Canada	4.00%	57.10	4.68		61.78	111.11	CAD	
China	–	4.00			4.00	4.00	SDR	d
Cote d'Ivoire	–	4.00			4.00	4.00	SDR	d
Czech Republic	–	4.00			4.00	4.00	SDR	d
Denmark	1.30%	18.56	1.52	5.00	25.08	25.08	SDR	d
Egypt	–	4.00			4.00	4.00	SDR	d
Finland	1.00%	14.28	1.17		15.45	20.86	EUR	c
France	7.02%	100.21	2.05		102.26	122.98	EUR	c
Germany	11.00%	157.03	12.86	1.41	171.30	171.30	SDR	d
Greece	0.05%	0.71	2.86		3.57	5.00	USD	
India	–	6.00			6.00	6.00	SDR	d
Ireland	0.11%	1.57	0.14		1.71	2.08	EUR	c
Italy	5.30%	75.66			75.66	82.53	EUR	c
Japan	18.70%	266.95	21.86	7.14	295.95	45,698.09	JPY	
Korea	0.23%	3.28	0.72		4.00	4.00	SDR	d
Luxembourg	0.05%	0.71	3.29		4.00	4.00	SDR	d
Mexico	–	4.00			4.00	4.00	SDR	d
Netherlands	3.30%	47.11	3.86		50.97	50.97	SDR	d
New Zealand	0.12%	1.71	0.14	2.15	4.00	10.35	NZD	
Norway	1.42%	20.27	2.02		22.29	220.00	NOK	
Pakistan	–	4.00			4.00	4.00	SDR	d
Portugal	0.12%	1.71	0.14	2.15	4.00	4.45	EUR	c
Slovak Republic	–	4.00			4.00	4.00	SDR	d
Spain	0.80%	11.42	2.55		13.97	13.10	EUR	c
Sweden	2.62%	37.40	3.06	1.14	41.60	450.04	SEK	
Switzerland	1.74%	24.84	2.03	5.10	31.97	31.97	SDR	d
Turkey	–	4.00			4.00	4.00	SDR	d
United Kingdom	6.15%	87.79	7.19	1.06	96.04	89.55	GBP	
United States	20.86%	297.78	9.14		306.92	430.00	USD	

Instrument for the Establishment of the Restructured
Global Environment Facility

Contributing Participants	Calculated Basic Contributions		Supplemental Contributions	Additional Supplemental Contributions	GEF-1 Total Contributions		
	(%)^a	SDR	SDR	SDR	SDR	Contribution^b	Currency
New Funding from Donors	89.80%	1,329.49	83.05	25.52	1,438.07		
Total					1,438.07	e	

** Based on Instruments of Commitment or Qualified Instruments of Commitment received by the Trustee.

a GEF basic share percentages are calculated based on new donor funding required for this replenishment in the amount of SDR 1,427.5 million.
    As agreed by the Contributing Participants in December 1992, the basic shares for IDA 10 were the beginning shares of all non-recipient donors to the GEF-1.

b Calculated by converting the SDR amount to the currency of contribution using an average daily exchange rate over the period from Feb 1, 1993 to Oct 31, 1993 as agreed by the Contributing Participants at the GEF-1 replenishment meeting.

c The contributions of these Contributing Participants that are member states of the European Economic and Monetary Union (EMU) were originally pledged in each of their legacy currencies. The Trustee converted these legacy currencies into EUR, the common currency for the EMU, in January 2000 at fixed conversion rates.

d These Contributing Participants denominated their contributions in SDRs.

e This is equivalent to USD 2.01 billion using the agreed reference exchange rates for the GEF-1.

COMMITMENTS

UPDATE TO GLOBAL ENVIRONMENT FACILITY TRUST FUND
SECOND REPLENISHMENT OF RESOURCES[1]

COMMITMENTS AS OF APRIL 30, 2007 **
(IN MILLIONS)

Contributing Participants	Calculated Basic Contributions (%)[a]	Calculated Basic Contributions SDR	Adjustment Toward Full Funding SDR	Additional Supplemental Contributions SDR	GEF-2 Total Contributions SDR	GEF-2 Total Contributions Contribution[b]	Currency
Australia	1.46%	21.95	1.52		23.47	43.27	AUD
Austria	0.90%	13.53	0.94 *c*	0.23 *c*	14.70 *j*	16.80	EUR *h*
Belgium	1.55%	23.30	1.62		24.92	30.94	EUR *h*
Canada	4.00%	60.13	4.17	10.30 *g*	74.60	141.66	CAD
China	_	4.00 *d*		2.00 *f*	6.00 *f*	6.00	SDR *i*
Cote d'Ivoire	_	4.00 *d*			4.00	4.00	SDR *i*
Czech Republic	_	4.00 *d*			4.00	4.00	SDR *i*
Denmark	1.30%	19.54	1.36		20.90	193.16	DKK
Finland	1.00%	15.03	1.04		16.07	19.63	EUR *h*
France	7.02%	105.54			105.54	131.50	EUR *h*
Germany	10.66%	160.32			160.32	198.99	EUR *h*
Greece	0.05%	0.75	0.05 *e*	3.20 *e*	4.00	4.46	EUR *h*
India	_	4.00 *d*		2.56 *f*	6.56 *f*	323.83	INR
Ireland	0.11%	1.65	0.12 *e*	2.23 *e*	4.00	4.69	EUR *h*
Italy	4.39%	65.97			65.97 *j*	73.85	EUR *h*
Japan	18.70%	281.13	19.54		300.67	48,754.33	JPY
Korea	0.23%	3.46	0.24 *e*	0.30 *e*	4.00	4,933.67	KRW
Luxembourg	0.05%	0.75	0.05 *e*	3.20 *e*	4.00	4.97	EUR *h*
Mexico	_	4.00 *d*			4.00	4.00	SDR *i*
Netherlands	3.30%	49.61	3.44		53.05	53.05	SDR *i*
New Zealand	0.12%	1.80	0.13 *e*	2.07 *e*	4.00	8.31	NZD
Nigeria	_	4.00 *d*			4.00	4.00	SDR *i*
Norway	1.42%	21.35	1.48		22.83	228.32	NOK
Pakistan	_	4.00 *d*			4.00	4.00	SDR *i*
Portugal	0.12%	1.80	0.13 *e*	2.07 *e*	4.00	4.90	EUR *h*
Slovenia	_	1.00			1.00	1.00	SDR *i*
Spain	0.80%	12.03			12.03	14.81	EUR *h*
Sweden	2.62%	39.39	2.73		42.12	448.07	SEK
Switzerland	1.74%	26.16	1.81	4.00	31.97	64.38	CHF
Turkey	_	4.00 *d*			4.00	4.00	SDR *i*
United Kingdom	6.15%	92.46	6.40	2.37	101.23	85.25	GBP
United States	20.84%	313.35			313.35	430.00	USD

Instrument for the Establishment of the Restructured
Global Environment Facility

Contributing Participants	Calculated Basic Contributions		Adjustment Toward Full Funding	Additional Supplemental Contributions	GEF-2 Total Contributions	
	(%)[a]	SDR	SDR	SDR	SDR Contribution[b]	Currency
1. New Funding from Donors	88.53%	1,364.00	46.76	34.53	1,445.30	
2. Carryover of GEF resources					500.63	k
Total (1 + 2)					1,945.93	l

** Based on Instruments of Commitment or Qualified Instruments of Commitment received by the Trustee.

a GEF basic share percentages are calculated based on new donor funding required for this replenishment in the amount of SDR 1,503.35 million. The basic shares, which are originally derived from the GEF-1 and largely maintained in the GEF-2, do not add up to 100%.
b Calculated by converting the SDR amount to the currency of contribution using an average daily exchange rate over the period from May 1, 1997 to Oct 31, 1997 as agreed by the Contributing Participants at the GEF-2 replenishment meetings.
c The Adjustment toward Full Funding and the Additional Supplementary Contribution are the result of encashing EUR 16.8 million on a five-year, rather than 10-year schedule.
d Represents the agreed minimum contribution level to the GEF-2.
e These Contributing Participants agreed to adjust their contributions upward to the minimum contribution level of SDR 4 million.
f China and India agreed to contribute more than the minimum contribution level of SDR 4 million.
g This represents a transfer of CAD 19.6 million (USDeq. 13.4 million) from a trust fund established by Canada during the pilot phase of the GEF.
h The contributions of these Contributing Participants that are member states of the European Economic and Monetary Union (EMU) were originally pledged in each of their legacy currencies. The Trustee converted these legacy currencies into EUR, the common currency for the EMU, in January 2000 at fixed conversion rates.
i These Contributing Participants denominated their contributions in SDRs.
j The SDR value of the contribution is enhanced as the result of an agreed accelerated encashment schedule.
k Represents the amount carried over to the GEF-2 valued on the basis of June 30, 1998 exchange rates.
l This is equivalent to USD 2.67 billion using the agreed reference exchange rates for the GEF-2.

Instrument for the Establishment of the Restructured
Global Environment Facility

UPDATE TO GLOBAL ENVIRONMENT FACILITY TRUST FUND
THIRD REPLENISHMENT OF RESOURCES[1]

COMMITMENTS AS OF APRIL 30, 2007 **
(IN MILLIONS)

Contributing Participants	Calculated Basic Contributions (%)[a]	Calculated Basic Contributions SDR	Supplemental Contributions SDR	GEF-3 Total Contributions SDR	GEF-3 Total Contributions Contribution[b]	GEF-3 Total Contributions Currency	
Australia	1.46%	27.60		27.60	68.16	AUD	
Austria	0.90%	17.01	0.69 c	17.70 g	24.38	EUR	
Belgium	1.55%	29.30	3.67 c	32.97 g	41.98	EUR	
Canada	4.28%	80.91		80.91	158.94	CAD	
China	_	4.00 d	4.44 c	8.44 fg	7.50	SDR	h
Cote d'Ivoire	_	4.00 d		4.00	4.00	SDR	h
Czech Republic	_	4.00 d	0.50 c	4.50 g	4.00	SDR	h
Denmark	1.30%	24.58	3.37	27.95	298.18 c	DKK	
Finland	1.00%	18.91	2.03	20.94	30.00 c	EUR	
France	6.81%	128.84 c		128.84	164.00	EUR	
Germany	11.00%	207.96	23.66	231.62	293.67	USD	
Greece	0.05%	0.95	3.55 c e	4.50 g	5.73	EUR	
India	_	4.00 d	3.99 c	7.99 fg	426.39	INR	
Ireland	0.11%	2.08	2.42 c e	4.50 g	5.73	EUR	
Italy	4.39%	82.99		82.99	118.90	EUR	
Japan	17.63%	333.41 c		333.41	48,754.33	JPY	
Korea	0.23%	4.35		4.35	5.51 c	USD	
Luxembourg	0.05%	0.95	3.05 e	4.00	5.73	EUR	
Mexico	_	4.00 d		4.00	5.07 c	USD	
Netherlands	3.30%	62.39		62.39	62.39 j	SDR	h
New Zealand	0.12%	2.27	1.73 e	4.00	12.14	NZD	
Nigeria	_	4.00 d		4.00	4.00	SDR	h
Norway	1.06%	19.96		19.96	228.32	NOK	
Pakistan	_	4.00 d		4.00	4.00	SDR	h
Portugal	0.12%	2.27	1.73 e	4.00	5.73	EUR	
Slovenia	_	1.00	0.13 c	1.13 g	1.00	SDR	h
Spain	0.80%	15.12		15.12	21.67	EUR	
Sweden	2.62%	49.53	7.45	56.98	764.67	SEK	
Switzerland	2.43%	45.94		45.94	99.07	CHF	
Turkey	_	4.00 d		4.00	4.00	SDR	h
United Kingdom	6.92%	130.82 c	19.09 c	149.91 g	117.83	GBP	
United States	17.94%	339.15 i		339.15	430.00 i	USD	

Instrument for the Establishment of the Restructured
Global Environment Facility

Contributing Participants	Calculated Basic Contributions		Supplemental Contributions	GEF-3 Total Contributions		
	(%)[a]	SDR	SDR	SDR	Contribution[b]	Currency
1. New Funding from Donors	86.07%	1,660.29	81.50	1,741.79		
2. Supplemental Contributions including Credits			12.50 c j	12.50		
3. Investment Income				104.47 k		
4. Carryover of GEF Resources				450.00 l		
Total (1 + 2 + 3 + 4)				2,308.76 m		

** Based on Instruments of Commitment or Qualified Instruments of Commitment received by the Trustee.

a GEF basic share percentages are calculated based on new donor funding required for this replenishment in the amount of SDR 1,890.5 million. The basic shares, which are originally derived from the GEF-1 and were largely maintained in the GEF-2, do not add up to 100%.

b Calculated by converting the SDR amount to currency of contribution using an average daily exchange rate over the period from May 15, 2001 to Nov. 15, 2001, as agreed by the Contributing Participants at the May 7, 2001, GEF-3 replenishment meeting.

c Contributing Participants had the option of taking a discount or credit for acceleration of encashment and; (i) including such credit as part of their basic share; (ii) counting such credit as a supplemental contribution; or (iii) taking such discount against the national currency contribution. France and Japan opted to include the credit for accelerated encashment in their basic share. The United Kingdom chose to accelerate encashment of its basic and supplemental contributions. A credit for accelerated encashment was thus included in its basic share and its supplemental contribution. Austria, Belgium, China, Czech Republic, Greece, India, Ireland, and Slovenia have opted to include the credit for accelerated encashment as a supplemental contribution. Denmark, Finland, Korea, and Mexico opted to take a discount against their national currency contribution. Canada chose to accelerate encashment of its contribution but not to take either a discount or a credit.

d Represents the agreed minimum contribution level to the GEF-3.

e These Contributing Participants agreed to adjust their contributions upward to the agreed minimum contribution level of SDR 4 million.

f China and India agreed to contribute more than the agreed minimum contribution level of SDR 4 million.

g The SDR value of the contribution is enhanced as the result of the agreed accelerated encashment schedule as noted in footnote c.

h These Contributing Participants denominated their contributions in SDRs.

i The United States pledged USD 500 million (representing a basic share of 20.86%) during the GEF-3 negotiations, of which USD 70 million was conditional upon achievement of the performance measures outlined in Schedule 1 to Attachment 1 of the GEF-3 Resolution. Such measures were not met.

j Represents (i) a credit from acceleration from Canada in the amount of SDR 10.13 million and (ii) a supplemental contribution from The Netherlands in the amount of SDR 2.37 million, bringing The Netherlands' total SDR contribution to SDR 64.76 million.

k The actual investment income earned on GEF resources during the GEF-3 commitment period (FY03 through FY06) was USD 132.46 million. This amount is converted to SDR using the agreed reference exchange rates for the GEF-3.

l Represents the amount carried over to the GEF-3 pursuant to paragraph 9 of Resolution No. 2002-0005, valued on the basis of June 30, 2002 exchange rates.

m This is equivalent to USD 2.93 billion using the agreed reference exchange rates for the GEF-3.

Instrument for the Establishment of the Restructured
Global Environment Facility

ATTACHMENT 1 TO RESOLUTION NO. 2006-0008

GLOBAL ENVIRONMENT FACILITY TRUST FUND
FOURTH REPLENISHMENT OF RESOURCES
TABLE OF CONTRIBUTIONS

CONTRIBUTIONS (IN MILLIONS)

Contributing Participants	GEF-4 Shares and Basic Contributions[a] (%)	GEF-4 Shares and Basic Contributions[a] SDR	Supplemental Contributions SDR	Adjustment Towards Full Funding SDR	Total Contributions SDR	Total Contributions Currency[b]	Total Contributions Currency
Australia	1.46%	24.43	6.61	-	31.04	59.80	AUD
Austria	0.90%	15.06	7.26 *c*	-	22.32	24.38	EUR
Belgium	1.55%	25.94	12.83 *c*	3.51	42.28	46.18	EUR
Canada	4.28%	71.62	17.57	-	89.20	158.94 *c*	CAD
China	-	4.00 *d*	3.10 *c*	-	7.10	9.51	USD
Czech Republic	-	4.00 *d*	0.68 *c*	-	4.68	142.89	CZK
Denmark	1.30%	21.75	11.68	1.32	34.75	310.00	DKK
Finland	1.00%	16.73	10.82 *c*	0.94	28.50	31.12	EUR
France	6.81%	71.28 *f*	57.42	-	128.70	188.71 *c*	USD
Germany	11.00%	115.05 *f*	86.08 *e*	-	201.14	295.00	USD
Greece	0.05%	0.84	4.41 *c*	-	5.25	5.73	EUR
India	-	4.00 *d*	2.72 *c*	-	6.72	9.00	USD
Ireland	0.11%	1.84	3.41 *c*	-	5.25	5.73	EUR
Italy	4.39%	73.46	-	-	73.46	87.91	EUR
Japan	17.63%	184.40 *f*	23.56	-	207.96	33,687.97	JPY
Korea	0.23%	3.85	0.62 *c*	-	4.47	6,142.97	KRW
Luxembourg	0.05%	0.84	3.16	-	4.00	4.79	EUR
Mexico	-	4.00 *d*	-	-	4.00	63.38	MXN
Netherlands	3.30%	55.22	19.47	-	74.70	89.38	EUR
New Zealand	0.12%	2.01	1.99	-	4.00	8.40	NZD
Nigeria	-	4.00 *d*	-	-	4.00	4.00	SDR *g*
Norway	1.44%	24.11	-	-	24.11	228.32	NOK
Pakistan	-	4.00 *d*	-	-	4.00	350.01	PKR
Portugal	0.12%	2.01	2.78	-	4.79	5.73	EUR
Slovenia	0.03%	0.50	3.88 *c*	-	4.38	1,146.20	SIT
South Africa	-	4.00 *d*	-	-	4.00	38.27	ZAR
Spain	1.00%	16.73	1.37	-	18.11	21.67	EUR

REPLENISHMENT

Instrument for the Establishment of the Restructured
Global Environment Facility

Contributing Participants	GEF-4 Shares and Basic Contributions[a]		Supplemental Contributions	Adjustment Towards Full Funding	Total Contributions		
	(%)	SDR	SDR	SDR	SDR	Currency[b]	Currency
Sweden	2.62%	43.84	24.70	7.66	76.20	850.00	SEK
Switzerland	2.26%	37.82	-	9.67	47.49	88.00	CHF
Turkey	-	4.00 *d*	-	-	4.00	4.00	SDR *g*
United Kingdom	6.92%	115.80	56.08	-	171.88	140.00	GBP
United States	20.86%	218.18	-	-	218.18	320.00	USD
New Funding from Donors	89.43%	1,175.34	362.22	23.10	1,560.66		
Projected Investment Income					250.91 *h*		
Projected Carryover of GEF Resources					325.67 *i*		
Total Projected Resources to Cover GEF-4 Work Program					2,137.23 *j*		

a   The GEF-4 basic shares reflect those of the GEF-3 except for Switzerland, Spain, Norway and Slovenia.

b   As agreed by the Contributing Participants at the June 9-10, 2005 GEF-4 replenishment meeting, the reference exchange rate to convert the SDR amount to the national currency will be the average daily exchange rate over the period from May 1, 2005 to October 31, 2005.

c   Contributing Participants have the option of taking a discount or credit for acceleration of encashment and; (i) including such credit as part of their basic share; (ii) counting such credit as a supplemental contribution; (iii) including such credit as an adjustment to full funding or (iv) taking such discount against the national currency contribution. Austria, Belgium, China, Czech Republic, Finland, Greece, India, Ireland, Korea and Slovenia have opted to take the credit for accelerated encashment as a supplemental contribution. Canada and France have chosen to take a discount against their contribution.

d   For those Contributing Participants that do not have a basic share, this represents the agreed minimum contribution of SDR 4 million.

e   Germany will provide this supplemental contribution of SDR 86.08 million under the terms of the GEF-4 replenishment resolution. This contribution will be made in order to strengthen the GEF's ability to meet funding objectives and policy commitments of the GEF-4 agreement. Progress towards meeting these commitments will be assessed in the GEF-4 midterm reviews and taken into account by Germany.

f   These contributions are calculated to reflect a replenishment share based on the contributions of several major donors.

g   As agreed by Contributing Participants in the June 9-10, 2005 GEF-4 replenishment meeting, Contributing Participants experiencing an average annual inflation rate in their economies exceeding 10% over the years 2002-2004 will denominate their GEF-4 contributions in SDR.

h   Investment income is projected using a USD 2 billion average cash balance and investment return of 4.6% per annum.

i   This amount comprises arrears, deferred contributions, and paid-in but unallocated resources.

j   This amount is equivalent to USD 3.13 billion using the agreed GEF-4 reference exchange rates.

Source: Instrument for the Establishment of the Restructured Global Environment Facility - March 2008, at http://www.thegef.org/gef/node/2552.

GEF-5 Contribution Table

Date: 28-Jun-10

Contributing Participants	Ccy	GEF-5 Basic Share, %	GEF-5 Actual Share, %	Total Contributions (in millions) SDR	USDeq	NC
1	2	3	4	15	16	17
Australia	AUD	1.46%	2.29%	52.88	81.03	105.00
Austria	EUR	1.21%	1.74%	40.15	61.53	42.60
Belgium	EUR	1.55%	3.33%	77.05	118.07	78.00
Brazil	USD	0.00%	0.35%	8.00	12.26	12.26
Canada	CAD	4.28%	5.85%	135.17	207.13	238.40
China	USD	0.00%	0.42%	9.79	15.00	15.00
Czech Republic	CZK	0.00%	0.20%	4.60	7.05	116.91
Denmark	DKK	1.30%	2.09%	48.40	74.16	400.00
Finland	EUR	1.00%	2.43%	56.20	86.11	57.30
France	EUR	6.76%	8.40%	194.16	297.52	215.50
Germany	EUR	10.89%	13.53%	312.64	479.08	347.00
Greece	EUR	0.05%	0.19%	4.35	6.67	4.44
India	USD	0.00%	0.28%	6.39	9.80	9.00
Ireland	EUR	0.11%	0.24%	5.62	8.61	5.73
Italy	EUR	2.89%	3.59%	82.89	127.02	92.00
Japan	JPY	11.48%	14.26%	329.55	505.00	48,377.08
Korea	USD	0.17%	0.23%	5.33	8.16	7.50
Luxembourg	EUR	0.05%	0.17%	4.00	6.13	4.44
Mexico	MXN	0.00%	0.28%	6.53	10.01	124.30
Netherlands	EUR	2.60%	3.23%	74.69	114.45	82.90
New Zealand	NZD	0.12%	0.17%	4.00	6.13	9.92
Nigeria	NGN	0.00%	0.17%	4.00	6.13	921.93
Norway	NOK	1.34%	1.66%	38.47	58.94	376.00
Pakistan	PKR	0.00%	0.17%	4.00	6.13	499.64
Portugal	EUR	0.12%	0.17%	4.00	6.13	4.44
Russian Federation	USD	0.00%	0.31%	7.10	10.89	10.00
Slovenia	EUR	0.03%	0.20%	4.71	7.21	4.80
South Africa	ZAR	0.00%	0.19%	4.35	6.67	51.56
Spain	EUR	0.97%	1.20%	27.76	42.54	30.81
Sweden	SEK	2.29%	3.70%	85.43	130.91	1,015.00
Switzerland	CHF	2.10%	3.26%	75.41	115.56	124.93
Turkey	TRY	0.00%	0.17%	4.00	6.13	9.57
United Kingdom	GBP	6.93%	9.28%	214.43	328.60	210.00
United States	USD	13.07%	16.23%	375.23	575.00	575.00
Total New Donor Funding		72.76%	100.00%	2,311.29	3,541.77	

		SDR	USDeq
1	**Total New Donor Funding**	**2,311.29**	**3,541.77**
2	Projected Investment Income	73.13	112.00
3	Projected Carryover of GEF Resources	448.27	686.55
4	Total Agreed Replenishment (1+2+3)	2,832.69	4,340.32

Source: CRS correspondence with GEF.

Figure A-2. Financial Status of GEF Trust Fund: Summary of Arrears

Countributing Participant	Repl.	Currency	Arrears Amount	USD eq.
Egypt	GEF-1	SDR	0.53	0.82
United States	GEF-2	USD	134.97	134.97
Nigeria	GEF-3	SDR	0.67	1.03
United States	GEF-3	USD	16.15	16.15
Spain	GEF-5	EUR	2.41	3.11
United States	GEF-5	USD	107.86	107.86
Total				263.93

Source: GEF, "Global Environment Facility Trust Fund Financial Report," GEF/C.43/Inf.08, September 30, 2012.

Author Contact Information

Richard K. Lattanzio
Analyst in Environmental Policy
rlattanzio@crs.loc.gov, 7-1754